T0056269

Arriving Well Activity Book is accompanied by a number of printable online materials, designed to ensure this resource best supports your needs.

The **Wellbeing Boost Game** and **Awards Ceremony** pages are available online to be downloaded and printed for easy use.

Go to https://resourcecentre.routledge.com/speechmark and click on the cover of this book.

Answer the question prompt using your copy of the book to gain access to the online content.

"The *Moving On* series gives all who work with children a powerful, practical tool to help them 'leave well so they can enter well'. As each book focuses on a particular stage of the moving process, children can find words and create images to express the often-paradoxical feelings any move can make. I highly recommend it!"
Ruth E. Van Reken, co-author of *Third Culture Kids: Growing Up Among Worlds*

Arriving Well Activity Book

Moving from country to country is no small feat. This activity book is designed for use with children aged 6–12 to help those on the move to navigate the process of global transition smoothly. Based on the latest relocation and transition research, wellbeing boosting strategies are shared for transition and beyond.

Children are introduced to mindful activities and are encouraged to use their creativity by annotating and illustrating the pages as they move through the book, allowing them to be an active participant in their move. *Arriving Well Activity Book* helps the child settle in their new place, to reflect on the move and understand that change is a part of life. Full of valuable strategies to boost wellbeing as they move forward, the text highlights top tips for settling in. The book normalises mixed feelings, helping the child to understand the process of transition and reflect on their sense of control. This book can be used effectively alongside:

Leaving Well Activity Book which helps children to reflect on how they feel about the move, to remember other moves and understand that change is a part of life.

Moving On Facilitator's Guide which offers guidance notes and prompts to help bring out the best experience for the child and is designed to help the adult feel confident in their delivery and in responding to any questions. It contains key points to consider, examples of 'what you could say', as well as explains the theory behind the workbook activities.

Acting as a tool for engagement, *Arriving Well Activity Book* will help children come to terms with the move and help adults support children through the arrival and settling in period.

Claire Holmes is Head of School Counselling at Tanglin Trust School, Singapore where she leads a team of counsellors who work across the whole school K-13. Claire's counselling modality is strength-based, empowering others to access their own inner wisdom and knowing. Her practice incorporates expressive therapies, mindfulness, and solution-focused interventions. In her role, she teaches mindfulness-based stress reduction (MBSR) to parents and staff.

Arriving Well Activity Book

Arriving Well Activity Book is part of a set – Moving On: Activity Books and Guide to Support Children Relocating to a New Country.

Book 1 – *Leaving Well Activity Book: Therapeutic Activities to Support Kids Aged 6-12 who are Moving to a New Country.*

Book 2 – *Arriving Well Activity Book: Therapeutic Activities to Support Kids Aged 6-12 who have Moved to a New Country.*

Book 3 – *Moving On Facilitator's Guide: How to Support Children Relocating to a New Country.*

Arriving Well Activity Book

Therapeutic Activities to Support Kids Aged 6-12 who have Moved to a New Country

Claire Holmes

Routledge
Taylor & Francis Group

LONDON AND NEW YORK

Designed cover image: Claire Holmes

First published 2024
by Routledge
4 Park Square, Milton Park, Abingdon, Oxon OX14 4RN

and by Routledge
605 Third Avenue, New York, NY 10158

Routledge is an imprint of the Taylor & Francis Group, an informa business

© 2024 Claire Holmes

The right of Author to be identified as author of this work has been asserted in accordance with sections 77 and 78 of the Copyright, Designs and Patents Act 1988.

All rights reserved. The purchase of this copyright material confers the right on the purchasing institution to photocopy or download pages which bear the copyright line at the bottom of the page. No other parts of this book may be reprinted or reproduced or utilised in any form or by any electronic, mechanical, or other means, now known or hereafter invented, including photocopying and recording, or in any information storage or retrieval system, without permission in writing from the publishers.

Trademark notice: Product or corporate names may be trademarks or registered trademarks, and are used only for identification and explanation without intent to infringe.

British Library Cataloguing-in-Publication Data
A catalogue record for this book is available from the British Library

ISBN: 978-1-032-46682-8 (pbk)
ISBN: 978-1-003-38282-9 (ebk)

DOI: 10.4324/9781003382829

Typeset in Tekton Pro
by KnowledgeWorks Global Ltd.

Printed in the UK by Severn, Gloucester on responsibly sourced paper

Access the Support Material: https://resourcecentre.routledge.com/speechmark

Dedication:

Dedicated to my companions on my global adventuring: My husband, Chris, my two Third Culture Kids, Hana and Ben, Neo the Scottie Dog, and Milo the tabby cat.

Acknowledgement:

These books would not have been possible without my International School journey, thank you Chris Holmes for initiating our overseas experience and what a blast it's been. Special acknowledgment goes to Hana Holmes for helping me reflect on content and layout; your creativity astounds me. Heartfelt thanks to my Tanglin Trust School Counselling Colleagues, past and present; Kendra Frazier, Valerie Hoglan, Paula Huggins, Pippa Gresham, Simon Parkin, Seunghee Chung, Jo Bush, Kevin Dunk, and Tash McCarroll; you have been unflagging sources of wisdom, inspiration, and compassion. Lastly, deep appreciation goes to my wonderfully wise School Counselling Supervisor, Helen Wilson, thank you for being my guru.

Welcome!

You've been given this activity book because you have moved to a new country.

It's a book that helps you learn about arriving well. Each page has a different activity. You'll get creative by drawing, colouring, writing, and making things. It will help you make a great start and settle in your new place.

This book belongs to _____

I have moved from _____ to

_____

Your life story.

Everyone's life story is unique (that means special to you). Below is your timeline, it stretches over to the next page. Add significant events like moving house, starting or moving to a new school, getting a new pet, siblings being born and/or visiting or moving to another country.

1. Write the event (the first one is done for you).
2. Below that, roughly the date or year the event happened.
3. Draw something that goes with the event underneath.

EVENT ➡️   was born

DATE/YEAR ➡️

DRAWING ➡️

Continue your timeline onto page 3

Change happens.

Change is a normal part of life; we've all been through transitions (which means moving from one thing to another). Put a star by the events that are transitions on your timeline. The last one is done for you.

*I
moved
to

Where are you now?

Draw something in the circle above to
represent your new country.

Feelings wheel.

Think of six of the biggest feelings you have experienced in your move.

Write one of them in each of the sections of the circle on the right. Colour each section of your feelings wheel.

Here are some feelings, you can probably think of more too:

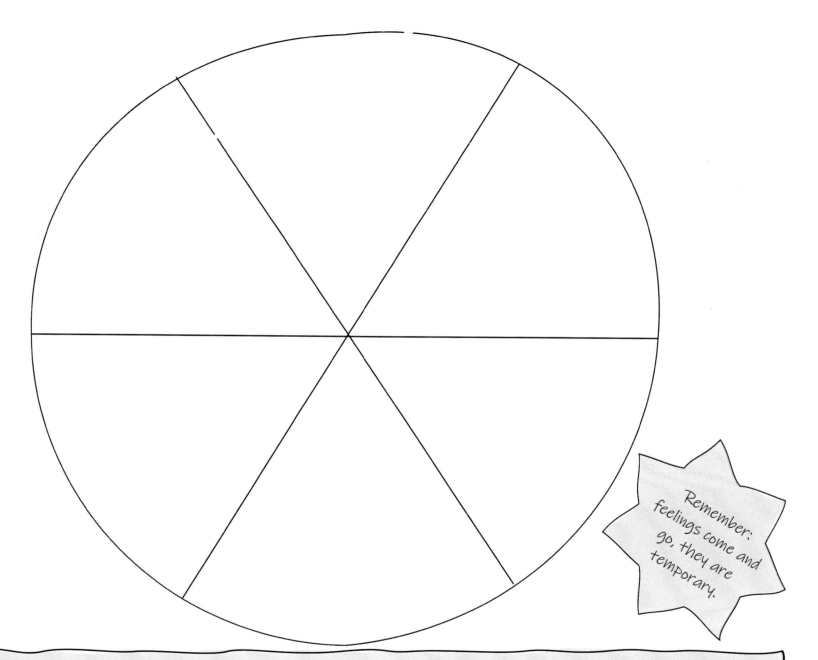

Remember: feelings come and go, they are temporary.

SAD ~ ANGRY ~ HAPPY ~ STRONG ~ LONLEY ~ UPSET~ EXCITED ~ CONFUSED ~ ENERGISED

Listen to your body and speak kindly to yourself.

Your body will let you know when big feelings arrive. Every body is different. Take each of your six big feelings from page 5 and draw symbols, colours, shapes, lines, or squiggles where you feel them in your own body inside the outline below. Add some labels to explain and any other details too.

What we say to ourselves impacts how we feel. Write a kind message to yourself in the thought bubble above. Make this your 'Arriving Well Message'. Repeat it silently and gently, as often as you need to.

Keep your breath in mind.

Your breath is a powerful tool. Paying attention to your breathing can help you feel in control in times of change. Repeat the Mountain Breathing instructions below five times (or more if you need to). Keep your finger on the page throughout.

Practise Mountain Breathing when you feel okay. When you get used to it try it when your body tells you big feelings have arrived.

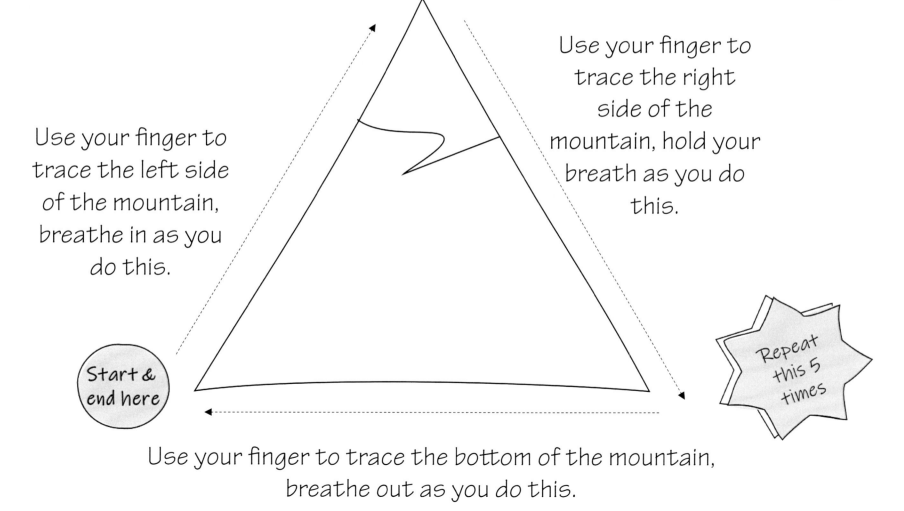

Use your finger to trace the left side of the mountain, breathe in as you do this.

Use your finger to trace the right side of the mountain, hold your breath as you do this.

Start & end here

Repeat this 5 times

Use your finger to trace the bottom of the mountain, breathe out as you do this.

Ground yourself.

Our minds can take us off into the future or the past. Being in the present moment helps us cope with change and make good choices.

54321 is a technique you can use to be present by using your senses.

Technique means a special way of doing something you can practise.

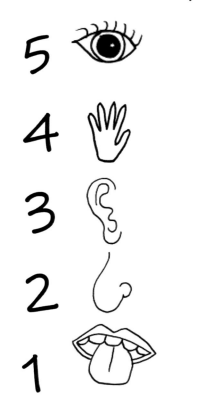

5

4

3

2

1

~Take a deep breath in and out ~

Notice and name...

5 things that you can see.

4 things that you can feel.

3 things that you can hear.

2 things that you can smell or smells that you like.

1 thing that you can taste or tastes that you like

~Take a deep breath in and out ~

Practise 54321 when you feel okay. When you get used to it, try 54321 when your body lets you know that big feelings have arrived.

Moving on graph.

Here is a graph showing how you might feel when you move from one place to another. The thin, jagged black line that runs through the middle represents your wellbeing.

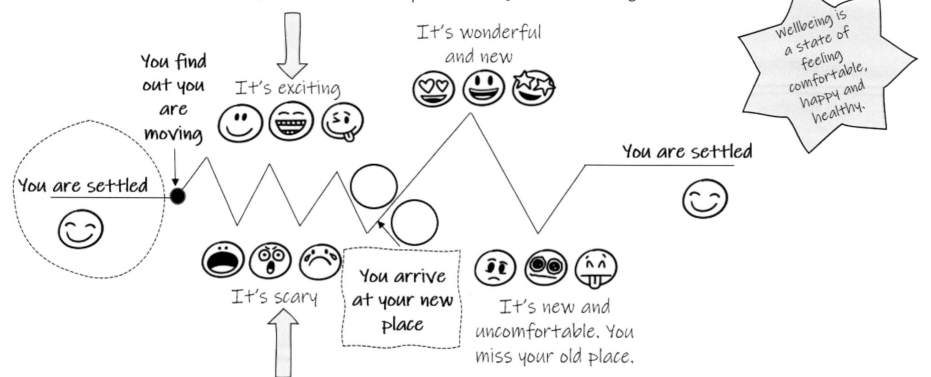

You find out you are moving

It's exciting

It's wonderful and new

You are settled

You are settled

Wellbeing is a state of feeling comfortable, happy and healthy.

It's scary

You arrive at your new place

It's new and uncomfortable. You miss your old place.

The circle, on the left, represents you before you knew you were moving. Most likely you were happy and okay most of the time. Then you heard you were leaving (represented by the black dot) which moved you along to the grey arrows, you probably felt excited and scared and a variety of other emotions too. Now you have landed in your new place, shown by the square on the graph.

Fill in the two blank emojis to show how you are feeling now. You can write the feeling next to them if you like. They can look the same or different to the others on the graph.

Pros (things that are going well) and
Cons (things that are not going so well).

Draw or write pros and cons of your new place in the boxes below:

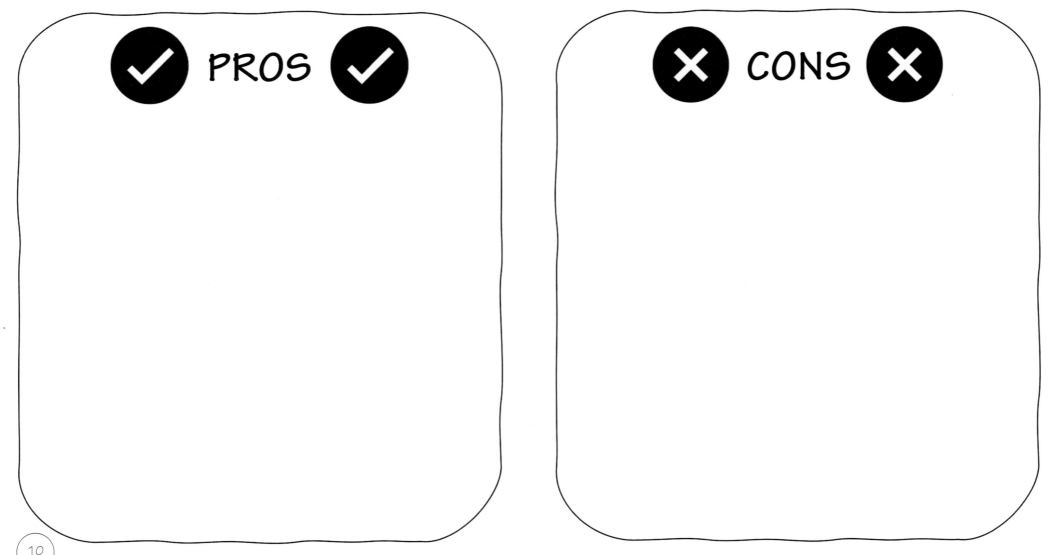

✔ PROS ✔

✖ CONS ✖

Mindful *colouring.*

Grab some pens or pencils and try mindful colouring. Take deep, slow breaths.

Try playing soothing music.

Doing something for you is important when things get busy.

Move your body to lift your mood.

Being active and moving your body helps you cope at times of change.

Write or draw ways of being active that you enjoy below:

Is there something active you enjoyed in your last place that you'd like to do here?

It was _____

Is there something new you'd like to try?

It is _____

The Magic of Vitamin N (N=NATURE)

Spending time in nature lifts your mood. A walk is a good way to be active in nature. Being still in nature also increases wellbeing. Caring for plants can be a great wellbeing boost too.

It's wonderful and new.

When most people arrive, everything is exciting and different. It's wonderful and new. This is shown on the graph below by the grey arrow.

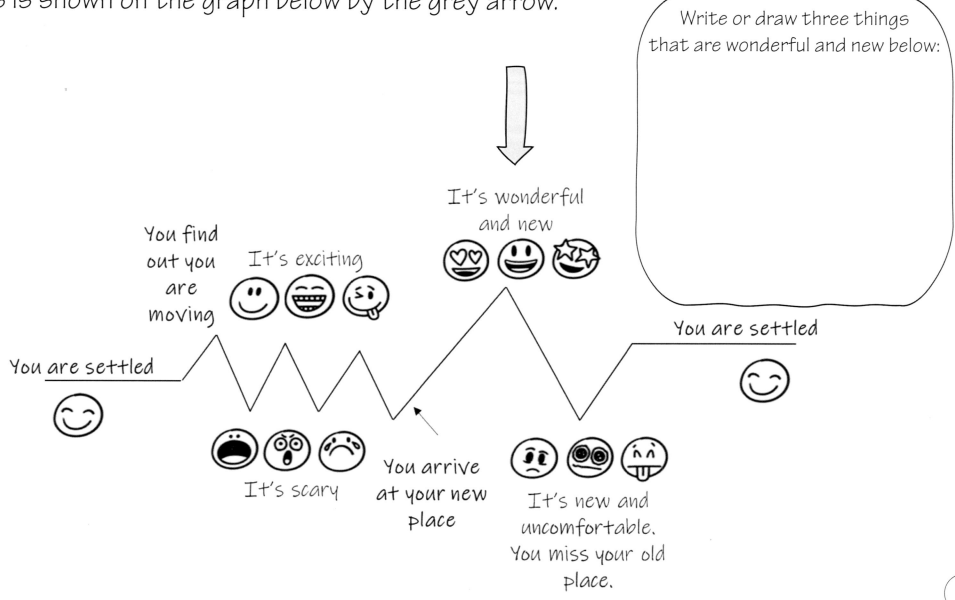

Write or draw three things that are wonderful and new below:

You find out you are moving

It's exciting

It's wonderful and new

You are settled

You are settled

It's scary

You arrive at your new place

It's new and uncomfortable. You miss your old place.

Missing where you came from.

After a while, you might miss where you came from and find yourself in 'the dip' shown on the graph by the grey arrow. Your wellbeing is likely to be lower than usual. You might feel angry or sad, or other emotions too. You may not feel like your 'usual self'. This is normal and part of building your new life. This 'dip' doesn't last for long; odds are you'll soon feel settled.

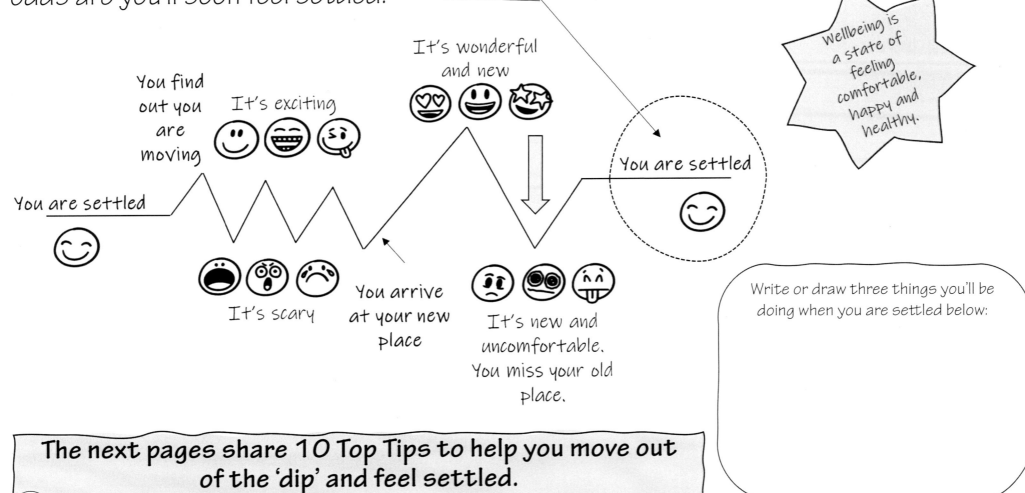

Wellbeing is a state of feeling comfortable, happy and healthy.

You find out you are moving

It's exciting

It's wonderful and new

You are settled

You are settled

It's scary

You arrive at your new place

It's new and uncomfortable. You miss your old place.

Write or draw three things you'll be doing when you are settled below:

The next pages share 10 Top Tips to help you move out of the 'dip' and feel settled.

Top tip # 1: Be brave.

Listen to your body, take deep breaths when you need to, and say things to yourself that help find bravery.

Draw colours, shapes, lines, and/or squiggles to represent bravery below:

Perhaps you'd like to add words too?

Remember your 'Arriving Well Message' from page 6 to help find bravery.

Top tip # 2: Be approachable and smile.

Make your body language approachable and open.

Stand up now and have a go!

Stand tall, press your feet into the floor, relax your arms by your sides, let your shoulders drop back and down, lift your chin, make eye contact and smile.

Use colours, shapes, lines, and/or squiggles to show what it feels like in your body to stand like this.

Top tip # 3: Keep curious.

Your new environment.

Keep curious about your new environment by asking questions. Here are some examples:

- Where's the library?
- What's the best club to sign up for?
- What's the best thing to eat in the canteen?

Tell people about yourself but don't forget to find out about others. One thing everyone loves to talk about is themselves. Get curious about your new classmates.

Write down some questions you could ask new friends about themselves below:

Most likely, you'll have fewer friends at your new school to begin with. As life goes on, there will be ups and downs, more friends, less friends; one thing is for sure, life keeps changing.

Top tip # 3: Keep curious.

New country report.

Imagine you are a journalist arrived in your new country. You are making a 'New Country Report'. Gather as much information as you can and add details to the squares below:

Three places to visit

What is the average temperature?

Draw the country flag

What language is spoken?

How do you say hello?

How do you say goodbye?

Three foods to eat

How many people live in this country?

Anything else you found out?

Top tip # 3: Keep curious.

Similarities and differences.

As you get curious, you'll discover things that are unique to your new country (only found here) and things that are unique to your old country (only found there). There will also be things that are the same in both. Fill in the circles below.

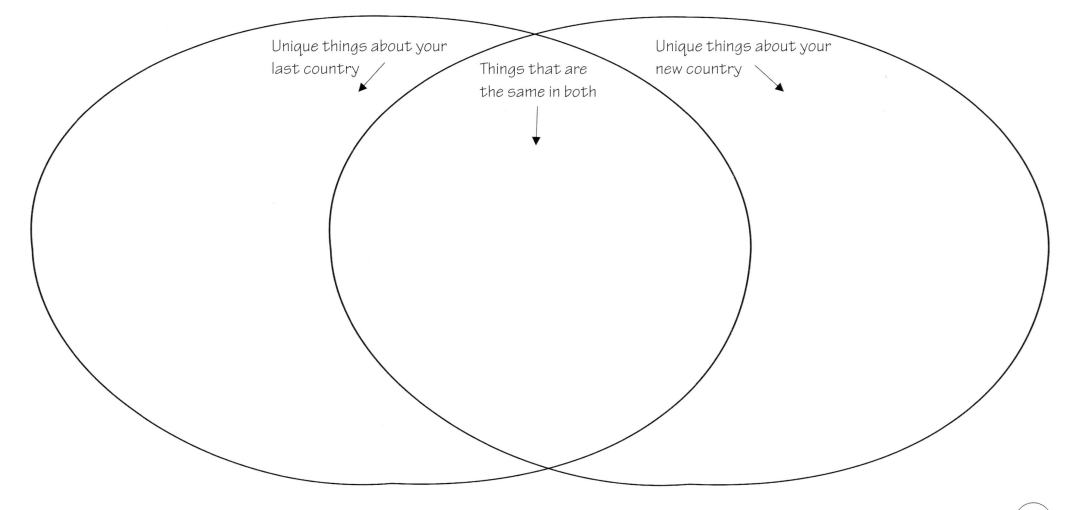

Unique things about your last country

Things that are the same in both

Unique things about your new country

Top tip # 4: Be yourself.

Be true to who you are. Let your brilliance shine.

Write five brilliant things about you below:

1) I am...

2) I am...

3) I am...

4) I am...

5) I am...

Say YES to opportunities and join in. Look for things that you love to do and try new things as well. Learning something new can boost wellbeing.

Top tip # 5: Be kind.

Kind to others.

Being kind not only benefits the person you are being kind to but also helps you feel better. Some ideas include: save someone a seat, say 'hi' in the corridor, give congratulations for a job well done, pay a compliment or notice when someone is upset, and ask them if they need help.

Write down or draw below some ways that you have been kind to others before:

Don't forget to be kind and helpful with your family, there's going to be a lot to do.

An act of kindness may cost nothing but may be the most valuable gift you can give.

Top tip # 5: Be kind.

Kind to self.

Being kind to yourself is important. Choosing to do things that bring you joy, nourish you, and help to relax boosts wellbeing. This will look different for everyone.

Draw or write things you can do that are kind to yourself when things are tough below:

Speaking to yourself kindly, like you'd speak to a good friend in key. Can you remember your 'Arriving Well Message' from P.6? Say it to yourself now.

You can also remind yourself that you are doing your best and settling in takes time.

Ask yourself at the end of each day 'What have I done to look after me today?'

Top tip # 6: Be grateful.

Being grateful helps to notice the good and what we notice we get more of. A way to do this is to notice three things every day that you feel grateful for. Bedtime may be a good time to do this. Draw three things you are grateful for in the hearts below. Write what it is underneath.

I am grateful for

_____

I am grateful for

_____

I am grateful for

_____

Top tip # 7: Focus on your strengths.

What are strengths?

Strengths are positive character traits that you and others notice. Using your strengths helps you be the best version of yourself.

Character traits are qualities that make you who you are.

Here are some examples of strengths:

Kind, caring, funny, patient, trusting, friendly, grateful, loyal, helpful, joyful, honest, determined, brave, creative, respectful, and peaceful.

Write other strengths you can think of here:

Top tip # 7: Focus on your strengths.

Strengths you take everywhere you go.

1) Write your strengths inside the body outline above.

2) In the box below, write three strengths you wrote in your body outline that are most important to help you arrive well.

3) In the box below, write one strength that you did not add to your body outline that would help you arrive well.

Top tip # 8: Remember your old place.

Most people like to stay connected with friends in their old place.
Write some ways you can do that below:

Put up photos and mementoes of where you moved from.

Fill in the 'memory' boxes below that help you remember your last place.
Use words or pictures:

Something I am proud of	A time I helped someone	Something that made me laugh

Top tip # 9: Make your bedroom a haven.

Make your bedroom (or part of a bedroom) comfortable and relaxing. This can help you feel settled. Draw or write things in the box below you have already added or would add to your space:

Haven means a special place where you feel safe and content.

Show this page to your parent/guardian to see what's possible.

Top tip # 10: Ask for help.

We all need help sometimes. Think of three people you can ask for help when things are tough. Write their names, one on each of the lines below the body outline that represents them. Feel free to make your people look more interesting by colouring them in.

_____   _____   _____

Write down any other supporters you can ask for help here:

Moving on podium.

Write down three things that you'd like to remember from this activity book in the boxes below.
Rank them 1–3, with 1 being the most helpful.

1

2

3

Instructions for making a 'Wellbeing Boost Game'.

Get ready:
Choose eight ways to boost your wellbeing (they are your Wellbeing Boosters).
Use the rectangles around this page to help you decide.

Make it (Go to page 31):
1) Write your eight 'Wellbeing Boosters' in the central triangles.
2) Colour in the colour triangles the same colour as their names (this is optional).
3) Cut out the whole square and turn its face down.
4) Fold each corner towards the centre so that the numbers and colours are facing you.
5) Turn it over and fold the corners to the middle so that you can see the colour names. Fold it in half so that the colour names are touching and the numbers are on the outside.
6) Open it and fold in half the other way.
7) Insert your thumb and first finger of each hand (pinching motion) under the number flaps.
8) Close the game so that only the number is shown.

Play it:
- Pick a number, open and close the wellbeing booster that number of times.
- Pick a colour and spell out the colour name, opening and closing the Wellbeing Booster for each letter.
- Choose a colour that you can see and open the flap.
- Read what it says and do it.

This can be played with one or two players and is a great way to remind yourself of what helps to boost your wellbeing.

Does drawing or colouring help you?

Is thinking of things you are grateful for helpful?

How could you move your body to release some energy?

What could you write down that would help?

Does splashing cold water on your face help?

Is there a breathing technique that helps?

Is something that you could eat or drink helpful?

Who could you talk to or hang out with?

What music could you listen to or play yourself?

What could you say to yourself?

Could making or creating something help?

Is there a toy or pet that might help?

Does standing or sitting up straight help?

What could you imagine that would feel calming?

Wellbeing Boost Game (instructions on the opposite page)

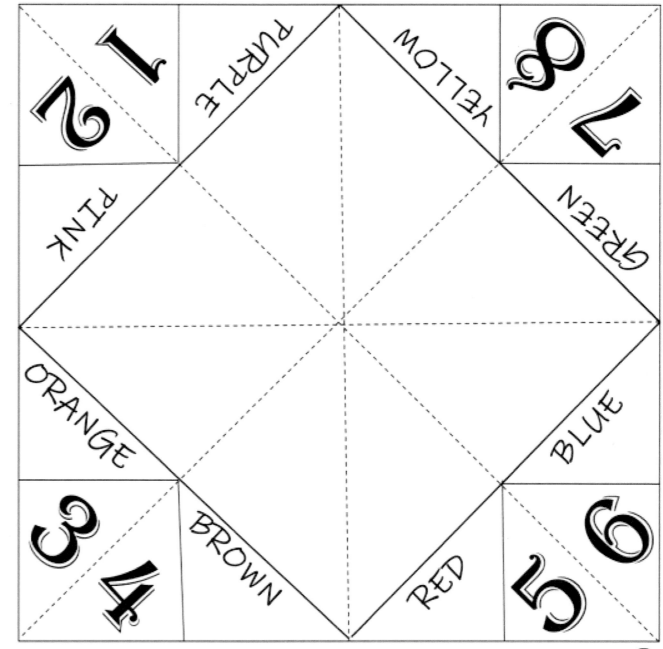

Awards Ceremony.

Read the stickers below. Choose a page that goes with each of them. Colour in the sticker, cut it out, and glue it onto your chosen page.

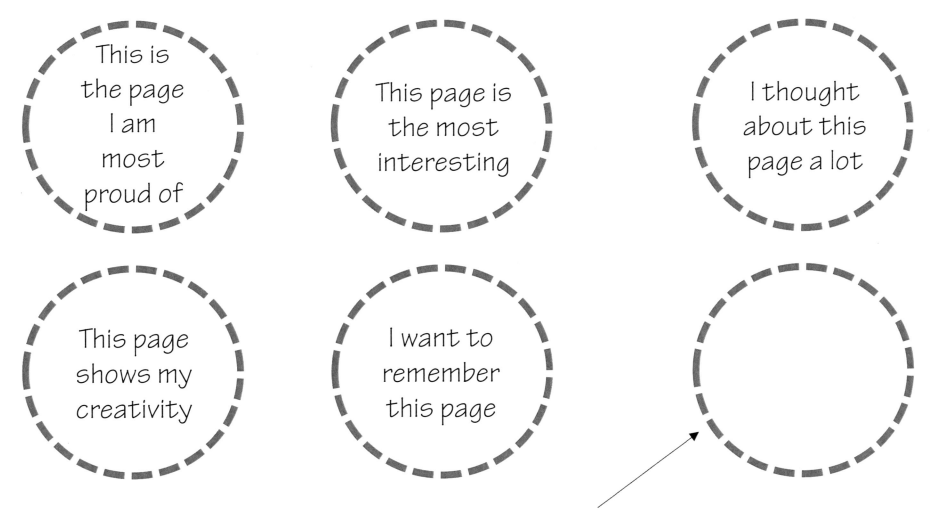

This is the page I am most proud of

This page is the most interesting

I thought about this page a lot

This page shows my creativity

I want to remember this page

Create your own sticker here

Copyright material from Holmes (2024), *Moving On: Arriving Well*, Routledge

'Brain-dump' page for any thoughts, scribbles, or notes: